POST-IMPRESSIONISM

★ IN MY GALLERY ★

WRITTEN BY
EMILIE DUFRESNE

DESIGNED BY
DANIELLE RIPPENGILL

Enslow
PUBLISHING

Published in 2022 by Enslow Publishing, LLC
101 W. 23rd Street, Suite 240,
New York, NY 10011

Designer: Danielle Rippengill
Editor: Madeline Tyler

Printed in the United States of America

CPSIA compliance information: Batch #CS22ENS: For further information contact Enslow Publishing, New
York, New York at 1-800-398-2504

Cataloging-in-Publication Data

Names: Dufresne, Emilie.
Title: Post Impressionism / Emilie Dufresne.
Description: New York : Enslow Publishing, 2022. | Series: In my gallery | Includes glossary
and index.
Identifiers: ISBN 9781978524194 (pbk.) | ISBN 9781978524217 (library bound) |
ISBN 9781978524200 (6 pack) | ISBN 9781978524224 (ebook)
Subjects: LCSH: Post-impressionism (Art)--Juvenile literature. | Post-impressionism (Art)--
France--Juvenile literature. |
Painting, French--19th century--Juvenile literature.
Classification: LCC ND547.5.P6 D843 2022 | DDC 759.05'6--dc23

IMAGE CREDITS

COVER AND THROUGHOUT – APRIL_PIE, SHTONADO, TASHANATASHA, QUARTA, DELCARMAT, SAMUI, MINII HO. BACKGROUNDS
– EXPRESSVECTORS. MAI & ARTISTS – GRINBOX. GALLERY – GOODSTUDIO, SIBERIAN ART. 5 – PRESNIAKOV OLEKSANDR,
NASTYASIGNE. 8 – EVERETT. 9 – DELCARMAT. 10&11 – EVERETT. 14&15 – ARDEAA. 18&19 – FREEEDA. 21 – VLADA YOUNG. 22&23 –
PHOTOGRAPHYJLMRTZ. 28 – ARDEAA, FREEEDA. 29 – PHOTOGRAPHYJLMRTZ. IMAGES ARE COURTESY OF SHUTTERSTOCK.COM. WITH
THANKS TO GETTY IMAGES, THINKSTOCK PHOTO AND ISTOCKPHOTO.

CONTENTS

Words that look like **this** are explained in the glossary on page 31.

WELCOME TO THE GALLERY

Hello and welcome! I'm Mai and I work in this gallery. I'm going to teach you all about Post-Impressionism. I'm also going to show you how to create some Post-Impressionist artwork in time for opening night.

Museums and Galleries

Museums and galleries are buildings that are used for showing art to the public. Some galleries and museums might buy art. Others might borrow art from other museums or galleries. By lending art to another museum or gallery, it means that people all over the world can see art from different times and places.

TYPES OF ART

There are lots of different types of art that an artist can create. Some of these include photography, assemblage or sculpture. The Post-Impressionists are known for their paintings. That means we need to know which words to use to help us describe paintings.

Impasto is when paint is layered thickly on a canvas so that it sticks out from the surface.

Brushstrokes are marks that are made with paintbrushes. Brushstrokes can be long and smooth or thick and short.

Palette knives are blunt tools that can be used for mixing paint or putting paint onto a canvas.

POST-IMPRESSIONISM WING

Welcome! The wing might not look like much just yet, but soon it will be filled with all the pieces of art that we will create in the style of Post-Impressionism.

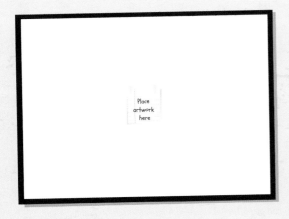

Place artwork here

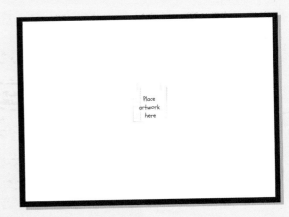

Place artwork here

Museums and galleries can have different rooms or areas. These different areas might have art from one specific artist or from a particular <u>movement</u> or time period. This gallery has lots of different wings that are <u>dedicated</u> to different art movements.

Post-Impressionist artists were mostly painters, so we need to make sure we have lots of frames on the walls to hang the paintings in. We need to paint these walls a plain color such as gray or white.

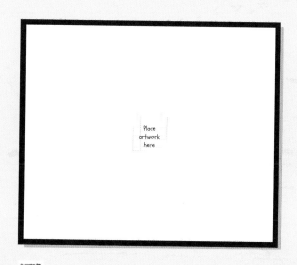

Place artwork here

MODERN GALLERY WALLS ARE OFTEN PAINTED WHITE. IT WAS AROUND THE TIME OF POST-IMPRESSIONISM THAT MANY GALLERIES BEGAN TO PAINT THEIR COLORFUL WALLS LIGHTER COLORS SUCH AS WHITE OR GRAY.

Now that we have the gallery set up, it's time to learn more about some Post-Impressionist artists and create some art.

WHAT IS POST-IMPRESSIONISM?

Before Post-Impressionism

The Post-Impressionists came after an art movement called Impressionism. The word "post" can mean "after." Impressionism was a very <u>revolutionary</u> art movement. These artists moved away from painting scenes from history or <u>mythology</u> and instead started painting people going about their everyday lives.

IMPRESSIONIST ARTWORK

IMPRESSIONIST ARTWORK

Instead of trying to show the world in a <u>realistic</u> way, the Impressionists wanted to show how one moment looked. Their paintings showed light and movement in new ways. At the time, this was very shocking, and Impressionism was seen as a new and different art form.

Moving Forward

By the end of the 1880s, Impressionism seemed less revolutionary. Some Impressionist painters began to push the ideas of Impressionism further and further. They kept some of the ideas of Impressionism but changed others.

POST-
IMPRESSIONIST
ARTWORK

Bold Brushstrokes and Colors

The Impressionists used short, thick brushstrokes with impasto. They also used a much brighter color palette. The Post-Impressionists, however, pushed this further, using even brighter colors and even bolder brushstrokes.

Express Yourself

In art, being expressive means showing or representing emotions rather than showing how something looks. The Post-Impressionists showed their emotions in lots of different ways, such as through the colors or shapes they chose, or how they put paint onto a canvas.

Getting Abstract

Post-Impressionist art also became more and more abstract. Abstract art is art that doesn't show how a thing might look in reality. Instead, the art might show an idea or a symbol of something. This means a color, shape, or image could be shown instead of a thing in real life. For example, a building might be shown as a flat square of color.

Important Individuals

Many of the Impressionists were friends. Lots of them created art in Paris and they often exhibited their work together. The Post-Impressionists did not all live in one area. Instead, most worked across all of France. This meant that different Post-Impressionist artists had very different styles.

FAUVIST ARTWORK

Pushing Art into the Future

Post-Impressionism was responsible for pushing art into more abstract and expressive places. Many people believe that Post-Impressionism inspired art movements such as Fauvism, Cubism, and Abstract Expressionism.

11

PAUL CÉZANNE

Country of Birth: France
Born: 1839
Died: 1906 (aged 67)

Paul Cézanne created many different styles of art throughout his lifetime, but he is best known for the works that were considered Post-Impressionist. As an artist, he began creating works that looked similar to classical art. During this time, he used very dark colors alongside light colors which he would put onto his canvas using a palette knife.

After this, Cézanne began to work with the Impressionist artist Camille Pissarro. Although this made his work more Impressionist, he still had a very different style than the Impressionist artists. Cézanne's work became more Post-Impressionist, and he began painting landscapes and still lifes. He was known for painting using simple, geometric shapes such as cylinders, cones, and squares, as well as using diagonal brushstrokes. It is because of the way he made his paintings out of geometric shapes that he is thought to have influenced Cubist artists such as Pablo Picasso.

13

Activity:
SHAPES AND STROKES

You will need:

A pencil ☑

Paintbrushes ☑

Paints in various colors ☑

Thick paper or cardboard ☑

It's time to create a Post-Impressionist landscape painting like Cézanne.

Find a picture of a nice area that has both buildings and plants in it. I have chosen this view of some houses on a hill.

Sketch out the basic shapes that make up the image. I'm sketching the buildings as squares and rectangles. I am drawing the tree trunks as cylinders and the tops of the trees as different circles.

Once you are happy with your sketch, it is time to paint. I am painting the buildings with block colors such as reds and browns. I will paint the trees and fields with lots of little diagonal lines in greens and browns.

Let your painting dry, and there you have it – a landscape painting in the style of Cézanne!

VINCENT VAN GOGH

Country of Birth: The Netherlands
Born: 1853
Died: 1890 (aged 37)

Vincent van Gogh only created art for a short amount of time. Despite this, he is seen as one of the most important Post-Impressionist artists of all time. Unlike other Post-Impressionists, van Gogh wasn't from France. He was from the Netherlands, so he was inspired by other artists who were from his country, such as Rembrandt van Rijn.

When he first started creating art in the 1880s, van Gogh mostly created watercolors and drawings. He was influenced by Impressionist art and Japanese art and he soon began working with paint. His style became very unique. He was known for his thick brushstrokes and impasto. He used bright and <u>pure</u> colors to express how he was feeling at the time. He was known for painting quickly and putting paint directly from the tube onto the canvas.

Activity:
SEEING MORE

You will need:

Thick paper or cardboard ☑

Paint in different colors ☑

Paintbrushes ☑

Tonight, I'm going to paint the night sky — just like van Gogh did!

Once it is dark, look out your window. What can you see? I can see the moon and a few stars dotted around it.

I am going to use short, thick lines to show how I am feeling. When I look out my window, I feel calm, so I am going to paint the sky with colors that make me feel peaceful, such as blues and purples.

The moon is a very bright yellow tonight, and orange around the edges – it looks quite unnatural. I will use bright yellows and oranges to show how different it looks from the sky. Around the moon and the stars I will also use lots of short, thick brushstrokes. This is because that is where I feel most of the energy is and those brushstrokes will help to show those feelings.

Once you have added all the colors and lines you want, let your painting dry. It's ready to show to people!

GEORGES SEURAT

Country of Birth: France
Born: 1859
Died: 1891 (aged 31)

Georges Seurat began painting alongside the Impressionists. However, even during the time the Impressionists were creating their art, his artistic techniques began to change. He still used bright colors and showed people socializing like the Impressionists did. However, he did not want to show a fleeting moment through light and movement.

Instead, Seurat and another painter, Paul Signac, began creating art in a completely new style. This style was called Pointillism. Pointillist paintings are made up of lots of small dots in different colors that come together to make a whole scene or image. From far away, the different-colored dots give the effect of different colors and shades depending on which colors you mix. Seurat would often paint landscapes or people outside using his Pointillist style.

POINTY PAINTING

You will need:

Thick paper or cardboard ☑

A pencil ☑

Paints in various colors ☑

Cotton swabs ☑

A camera ☑

It's time to make a pointy painting, just like Seurat. Let's get dotty!

Go to an outside place such as a park or the beach, or anywhere where people are sitting outside. Take a photo so that you don't forget how it looks.

Using the photo, sketch out the scene. Once you are happy with your sketch, it is time to get painting. Use your cotton swabs to make tiny dots on your sketch. Use different cotton swabs for different colors so that the paint doesn't mix. You can use whatever colors you want – they don't have to be the ones you see in the photo. I'm using greens and browns for mine.

Once your painting is dry, stand back from it and see how the dots create different shades of colors and make the whole painting look complete.

ÉMILIE CHARMY

Country of Birth: France
Born: 1878
Died: 1974 (aged 96)

Émilie Charmy began painting in her early life and continued into her 90s. She painted through many different movements including Impressionism, Post-Impressionism, and Fauvism.

Although she changed her artistic style slightly to fit in with these movements, she always had a style that was obviously her own. She was known for her portraits of women and she would change her style to fit the different moods or settings of each woman. Much like other Post-Impressionists, she used bright colors and lots of different brushstrokes to create different textures. For example, in her painting *Woman in Armchair*, Charmy used a palette knife to create the heavy folds in the woman's velvet dress.

Unfortunately, Charmy did not receive much fame in her lifetime. However, her works show her to be a very revolutionary painter who broke rules and <u>conventions</u> for the time she was living in.

Activity:
PECULIAR PORTRAITS

You will need:

Thick paper or cardboard ☑

A pencil ☑

Paint in various colors ☑

Paintbrushes ☑

Plastic or old knife ☑

Sponges ☑

Let's paint a portrait in the style of Charmy.

First, you need to find someone to paint a portrait of. I am painting myself, but you could ask a family member or someone you are close to. Get them to stand or sit while you sketch and paint them.

First, sketch out the basic parts of their face and clothes. Once you are happy with your sketch, it is time to paint. Look at your model and think about what they might be feeling. Do they seem happy or sad, relaxed or tense?

Choose colors and tools that you think show how your model is feeling. I am using sponges for the background.

Now I just need to choose a few more colors. I might use the palette knife to paint the hair and then short, thick brushstrokes for the face.

OPENING NIGHT

Wow – look at our Post-Impressionist art now that it is up on the walls! Everyone is talking about the artwork. Let's listen in and see what they think.

I love how simple the shapes and brushstrokes are.

The grass in the fields really feels like it is moving. It makes me feel peaceful.

I love it. There is so much movement and imagination. I am going to look at the sky differently now.

Do you like this one?

You don't have to like every piece of art, but it is good to talk about what we do and don't like about different artworks and how they might make us feel. Everyone's opinions and thoughts are important.

This one is very different than the other paintings, but it is a very interesting style.

What do you think of the paintings you have created? Which one is your favorite? How does each piece make you feel?

I'm not sure I like this one. The brushstrokes make me feel uneasy.

Really? They make me feel calm.

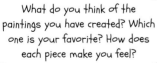

QUIZ

1. What art movement came before Post-Impressionism?
2. What three art movements is Post-Impressionism thought to have influenced?
3. Which Post-Impressionist painter was born in the Netherlands?
4. What art technique involves painting lots of tiny dots next to each other?
5. Which artist painted *Woman in Armchair*?

Answers: 1. Impressionism **2.** Fauvism, Cubism, and Abstract Expressionism **3.** Vincent van Gogh **4.** Pointillism **5.** Emilie Charmy

Have you ever been to a museum or gallery?

Why not go to a museum or gallery to have a look at some art? Try to think about how each painting makes you feel and why. It might be interesting to see what other people think of the art. Does how they feel about the art change how you see it?

GLOSSARY

Abstract Expressionism	an art movement where art became more abstract and more expressive
assemblage	a type of art that can look like sculpture or an installation in which different objects are assembled together to make one whole piece
canvas	a woven fabric that is pulled tightly over a frame to create a blank space to be painted on
classical art	art that shows the ancient Greek and ancient Roman civilizations
conventions	the ways of doing things that are accepted by a large number of people
Cubism	an art movement in which people and objects were represented through geometric shapes such as cubes
dedicated	in honor of one particular person or cause
Fauvism	an art movement that was very expressive and used unnatural colors
influenced	to have had an effect on the behavior of someone or something
inspired	to be influenced to do something
landscapes	scenes that include nature, such as fields, mountains, or oceans
movement	a category or type of art that an artwork or artist might belong to, sometimes related to a certain time or place
mythology	the myths and legends of different cultures
palette	the colors that an artist or a group of artists might use or the board on which an artist might mix their paint
photography	a type of art that uses cameras to take photographs of landscapes, people, or things
pure	not mixed with anything else, such as another color
realistic	looking as though it is from the real world
revolutionary	doing something in a way that drastically changes how it was done or thought of before
sculpture	a decorative object made by carving, chiseling, or molding
sketch	to do a quick drawing, often in pencil
still lifes	paintings or drawings of objects that aren't living, such as fruit, bottles, bowls, and glasses
symbol	something that stands for, or means, something else

INDEX